POSITIVE RESULTS

True Stories of Inspiration and Hope for Cancer Fighters and Caretakers

ANDREW MCALEER

ABOUT POSITIVE RESULTS

In August 2005, less than two years after losing his mother and father to cancer—dying six days apart—Andrew McAleer was diagnosed with fourth-stage melanoma. Less than three years later, at age forty-one, fulfilling a lifelong dream to serve his nation, he graduated from Army Basic Combat Training. At age forty-four, holding the rank of sergeant, he would go on to complete a tour of duty in Afghanistan as a U.S. Army Historian. A few months after returning from Afghanistan, McAleer was again diagnosed with fourth-stage melanoma. This time four doctors told him it was inoperable. In *Positive Results*, Andrew McAleer shares his personal, heartfelt, and inspiring stories about his fifteen-year battle with cancer, first as a caretaker and then as a patient.

ABOUT THE AUTHOR

Mr. McAleer is the author of numerous books, including the *101 Habits of Highly Successful Novelists*, *A Miscellany of Murder* (co-author), *Double Endorsement*, *Fatal Deeds* and a co-editor and contributor to the Coast to Coast anthology series published by Down & Out Books. Past president of the Boston Authors Club, Mr. McAleer teaches at Boston College's prestigious Woods College and works in public service as a labor relations specialist. Holding the rank of sergeant, he served in Afghanistan as a U.S. Army Historian. Visit him at: www.amcaleer.com

PRAISE FOR POSITIVE RESULTS

"Using skills honed as a mystery writer, each chapter of Andrew McAleer's *Positive Results* grabs the reader and unrolls a vivid story of his true battles with cancer. Every oncologist and cancer patient – hell, anyone who wants to see what being fully alive means—must read this book."

—**John Merrifield**, M.D. author of *Abby's Deal*

"Andrew McAleer's *Positive Results* is one of the most inspiring, motivating, and heartfelt books I have ever read and re-read! This heroic memoir will remain within me forever."

—**Thomas Donahue**, author of *Fraternal Bonds*

"*Positive Results* is the truly remarkable account of McAleer's fight to survive against all odds. An amazing, amazing journey readers must take with him."

—**Kris Meyer**, Producer, *The Lost Son of Havana* and Executive Producer *Plimpton! Starring George Plimpton as Himself*

To

Mrs. Enid Kelly

and

David "Sir Gov" McGovern

Two of the Many Brave Fighters on Many Fronts

CONTENTS

BOOKS

BY ANDREW MCALEER

The 101 Habits of Highly Successful Novelists

Mystery Writing in a Nutshell
(Co-Author)

Coast to Coast: Private Eyes from Sea to Shining Sea
(Co-Editor)

Coast to Coast: Murder from Sea to Shining Sea
(Co-Editor)

Fatal Deeds

Double Endorsement

A Miscellany of Murder
(Co-Author)

Packed and Loaded: Conversations with James M. Cain
(Compiler)

The Jane Austen Chapbook of Wit and Wisdom
(Compiler)

ONE

The Grass Door

Life is too short to be little.
–Disraeli

Cancer could kill me, but not destroy

me. On a bitter cold, rainy day in March,

2014, I felt a prescient need to buy my own

eternal resting site. This despite being only in

my mid-forties and receiving a call from my

latest and bravest cancer surgeon scheduling what we hoped would be a life-saving surgery in just ten days. I had ten days to get the job done. Time, as the saying goes, "is of the essence."

About a year prior—a few months after returning from an eleven-month tour in Afghanistan, after joining the army three years prior, at age forty-one—doctors had diagnosed inoperable fourth-stage melanoma. My second lymphatic battle with this particular enemy in less than a decade. The latest tumor blew up in a lymph node running laterally from my right pelvis into my bladder, and grew to the size of a cantaloupe, latched onto my femoral artery, and enveloped a web of veins. My doctor told me as it grew, the tumor pushed the artery into my bladder. I remember peering intently at the pet scan, the little bugger had pushed so deep into my bladder that my squashed bladder took on the shape of a sausage.

Four doctors told me the artery and vein business made the surgery a no go. A radiologist told me the tumor had plastered itself to my pelvic bone and that radiation would be a waste of time. Even with my limited understanding of medical terminology,

I surmised that having an inoperable, malignant tumor that wouldn't respond to radiation cloistered in my pelvic bone, could prove problematic.

Luckily, my particular mutation allowed me to take an oral round of heavy-duty chemo. Eight horse pills a day, lots of wild Maine blueberries, and five months later, the tumor shrank approximately 45 percent. I rounded that up to 50 percent, but despite my mathematical wizardry, the latest surgeon still wouldn't yank that sucker out. So I pulled up my tent pegs and found one willing to take a stab at it, even though he offered no guarantees. So who does? The bottom line, I had no choice—it was radical surgery or die.

So, as someone used to handling the details of my life with efficiency, a few weeks before facing surgery, I met up with a polite young woman named Beth to negotiate the purchase of a cemetery plot. We met at the Mayflower Cemetery located in Duxbury, a swell community near Plymouth, also founded in the 1600s, on the south shore of Massachusetts. Although I arrived an hour early, Beth greeted me like one might an old friend, grabbed her car keys and a large, wax-coated plot plan of the cemetery, and beamed a genuine smile. "Let's take a look," she said, looking a tad disconcerted to discover a man so young—and healthy looking—somewhat urgently shopping for his own plot.

Beth and I chatted with ease as she wended her sedan over the familiar, narrow lanes of the cemetery. When we stopped on Evergreen Lane, nodding towards my Army hat, Beth told me her father had served in the First Infantry Division—known as the Big Red One in World War II and Korea.

"You're kidding me," I said, "I was attached to the Big Red One in Afghanistan. Is your dad still alive?"

"He died in 2002," Beth told me. "He'd be ninety-nine if he was still alive."

"If he served with the Big Red One, he would've been in virtually every major WWII campaign," I said. I thought about my own father who enlisted in the Army in WWII at the age of nineteen. Like many GIs, he brought a small sack of American soil with him overseas. In the event he died, a battle buddy could sprinkle a bit of the homeland over his grave.

"He ended up in Japan. I'm half Japanese," Beth offered. "My father met my mother while he was there training for Korea, and it took them a year and half to get permission to marry." Neither government approved of the marriage, she told me.

Her father eventually received permission from the two warring nations to marry his sweetheart, who had undoubtedly survived a few blood baths of her own. They moved to America and raised the lady who was now making my present business remarkably peaceful.

Next to this portion of Evergreen Lane stood a mature oak in a matted, scraggly lawn covered with scatterings of winter debris and brush. I tried to imagine nothing but manicured green grass surrounding the healthy crop of American veteran memorial flags on the graves of deceased veterans. Sooner or later I could be their neighbor. I was banking on later, but then again, maybe I wasn't.

I waved my hand over the area and tried not to sound too eager. "Anything here?"

Beth examined the waxy plot plans as near-frozen drops of rain beat like the drums of time against its surface. She looked up. "There're three available here."

It was time to get down to brass tacks.

"How much for a plot?"

"They're $600 for residents."

Although my family had had a vacation home in the area for decades, I could claim only summer residency. No time like the now to negotiate for permanent status. "I'm a summer resident. That count?"

"It sure does."

I put in my order. "I'll take two."

Maybe I made an impulsive purchase. Did I really need two? Perhaps, I might get married someday and heaven forbid I get caught a grave short. Back at the office, Beth gave me a list of headstone businesses and some literature outlining the rules and

regulations of the Mayflower Cemetery.

Suppressing an urge to salute, I dutifully

agreed to obey the rules and regs when the

time came. After a hug from Beth, I walked

away with an official Certificate for Burial

Rights making me the proud owner of No.

1555A Graves 3 and 4. In some strange way I

felt relieved for taking care of this detail and

not shoving it aside for the living. I headed

over to one of the best bakeries on the south

shore, French Memories in Duxbury's Snug

Harbor, for some heavy-duty pastry. I

ordered a flaky, buttery looking item

containing a fat dollop of homemade apricot preserve in the center called a "sunburn." The smell of fresh coffee, fresh breads and pastries filled my lungs. The senses alive and well here and ready to partake in whatever's left. This was the sort of five minute vacation my mother loved and deserved more of.

While watching the rain pummel the bakery windows, I texted my buddy Vince to see how he was doing. I made no mention of what I was up to, just that I had taken a personal day off work. Next, I shot over to the Coffee Shack in Green Harbor for coffees. Afterwards, I drove to my brother

Paul's place in Green Harbor, where we talked about the latest "cool" movies, the economy, one of our favorite shows of all time—Magnum P.I.—and an old cartoon called Tennessee Tuxedo, all part of our usual brother chit-chat. Anything but the reality of buying a cemetery plot a week before my life-or-death surgery. No one, especially me, wanted to belabor the situation. Best to buck up and carry on.

From there, I swung by my friend Tom's ice cream store, Nona's in Hingham, where he sold me—insisting on a military discount—a sundae floating in freshly made whipped cream. Despite the pastry and all those coffees, I lapped it up, realizing that—if I lived—I'd be working off that treat until I passed at a much later, far-more-appropriate stage of life.

The ride north to Lexington went smoothly (no Cape traffic heading north on Route 93 traffic to slow me down), and when I arrived home, I caught the end of the Red Sox/Orioles game with my brother Jay. The Sox lost, but a new season had begun and with that a hope of victory. Despite the cold rain and the anticipation of the physical and emotional challenges ahead, that last day in

March was good to have and I wouldn't give it back. Not without a fight. I took care of necessary business, met Beth, paid respect to some of the men and women who gave their lives to make this country great, and connected with the ones I cared most about.

People who claim to be in the know say you can't take it with you when you die. I'm not so sure. The big brothers, the friends, the comfort zones, the little things that matter like an extra dollop of whipped cream with the kindness of a military discount are all here for the taking. And, if it happened to be my time to go, when that torn earth above me finally healed and that grass door closed on me for good, they'd be there still. I could live with that.

**

TWO

The Accidental Caretaker

You cannot prevent the birds of sorrow from flying over your head, but you can prevent them from building a nest in your hair.

—Chinese Proverb

Part I

John "Dad" McAleer

My father died November 19, 2003,

ending a ten-year battle with non-Hodgkin's

lymphoma. He was eighty. My mother died

six days later, after a two-year, heroic battle

with breast cancer. She was seventy-eight. As

much as we wish our mothers and fathers

would never die, they do. Before mine did,

however, I got to know them—and their

hair—at a deeper level of intimacy.

All their lives, even at the end, my

mother and father both had beautiful heads of

hair. That devil cancer never got his hands on

either head—but I did. I had the good fortune

of becoming my parents' primary caretaker

through the last eighteen months of their

lives, which often proved challenging and left

27

me struggling to endure the stress and sadness that came with observing and steadying them through their declines. Still, we shared a lot of personal joys and thoughts that otherwise would have been lost had they been allocated to a far more impersonal wing of a nursing home. Not that nursing homes are necessarily deficient—some try very hard to offer nurturance and I worked in one for six years alongside some of the most dedicated people in health care—but, if we can provide it, the parent/child bond that forms at birth can come full circle when a child tends to an ailing parent. Perhaps nothing teaches us more about life and death.

And thus I willingly took on the care of my ailing parents, both of whom were battling cancer. One day, just days before the end of his life, my father wasn't up for showering. I didn't really understand depression at the time, particularly when—no matter how tired or sick he clearly felt—he always forced a smile and shared one of the many humorous stories he accumulated throughout his life. Luckily, however, I had the kind of sense that comes from a family deeply rooted in New England for generations and knew not to pressure him too hard.

"Okay, Sergeant," I said, giving him back his WW II rank, "just means more USO dames for me."

Dad thought for a moment then rallied. "Maybe I can manage."

I warmed the water flow to a safe temperature and then lifted my once strong father onto the shower chair. He looked at his wasted body and joked, "Careful you don't cut yourself on my bones."

To distract us both from the stunning visual, I briskly lathered up his body until he looked like a snowman and then sprayed him off with a rush of warm, pulsating water, followed by a quick shave to render his sideburns crisp and square. I then wrapped my ailing father in fresh towels and placed one hand on his shoulder as we strolled the four feet back to his bedroom. After applying lotion to his skin, with an extra order for his feet, I patted both of his freshly shaved cheeks with a brisk aftershave and helped him dress in comfortable clothes, right down to his 1950-esque slippers.

"Thank you," Dad said, after getting him settled into his favorite wing chair. "I'm glad you convinced me to do that. I feel so much better."

I uttered something incredibly insightful like, "No problem."

Then we turned to his hair, which had reached that perfect dampness for combing. Because he had opted for an antibody known as Rituxan instead of chemotherapy to treat his cancer, even at age eighty, Dad still possessed a good crop of hair. And it still boasted about fifty percent of that rich brown I'd known him to have all my life, up until his illness. It also still had the same natural curls and pods of cowlicks. In the 1970s, he'd worn it long, accented by thick sideburns. In photos, it gave him the kind of cool look any professional hockey player from the 1970s would have been proud to take for a tour around the ice. But, oddly enough, my father never brushed those thick locks. You see, my father was a little-black-comb type of guy.

Dad would generally have at least three items on him at all times: an ironed handkerchief, a book, and a little black comb. In a sauna. Emerging from the ocean. In a country where tyrants outlawed such items. No matter where my father went, he'd somehow manage to be packing these three necessities. To be clear, I'm not saying he didn't carry a wallet or car keys, just that, as an absent-minded professor, it would be unusual for him to be in possession of both his wallet and car keys at any given time.

I admired the hell out of my father. It took ten years of cancer, countless surgeries, experimental treatments, and something called Gram-negative pneumonia to reduce my father to his weakened condition. He put the "gentle" in gentleman, always offering a kind word, always a kind, interesting story. He had a genuine way of making everyone he met feel important and purposeful—because he viewed everyone as important and purposeful. A few days after he died, my father's oncologist called me. He wanted me to know that in all the years he'd been treating my father, that my father would refuse treatment during the school year because he didn't want the treatment to interfere with his teaching. "The only thing that mattered to your father," he told me, "were the students."

As I combed my father's hair that October morning he said to me, "I wish I'd shown as much patience with my father when he was dying as you do with me." I knew this not to be the case. True to form, even in his weakened condition he was trying to find a way to elevate others. I didn't know what to say, so pretended not to hear the man I'd admired all my life. The man, who sixty short years ago, made it through Army Basic Combat Training with flat feet. I focused instead on using his little black comb to direct every hair into its proper slot. I wanted him to look and feel sharp. I wanted him to feel as proud of himself as I did.

***

THREE

The 800-Pound Saltine

Better to light one candle than to
curse the darkness.
—Old Chinese Proverb

There wasn't a chance in hell I'd let

something as small as a saltine lick me. I'd

admit I had doubts about who would lick

whom, and maybe I was just talking tough,

but in the end it went down. Not without a

damn good fight though. I'd give it that.

The fight began as I sat on the edge of my bed, in February 2006, quickly dissolving into a swamp of depression. It was dark, in the cold, witching hour of the night. My brother Jay and I lived together in an old farmhouse and had never upgraded to triple-pane-double-sealed-vacuum-sealed windows or whatever they're selling these days. We had (still have) old, rattling storm window jobbers. I'm convinced they called them "storm windows" not because they keep the stormy New England winters out, but because they let them in, under the quilt and into the marrow of your bones. I knew without looking at the clock that dawn was a million minutes away. I knew because every night was the same drill. I couldn't sleep and couldn't stay awake either. Time moved at the pace marble turns to dust.

The anxiety and nausea throttled into overdrive as it had, it seemed, since the beginning of time. The notion of ever having enjoyed food or a peaceful night's sleep had been completely erased from my memory bank. I mean completely. I honestly could not fathom that I had ever enjoyed pizza, prime rib, potato chips, or even Mom's apple pie. Or

that I had ever hit the pillow after a hard day's
work and calmly dozed off to sleep, excited to
fall asleep lickety split, so that magical, fast-
forward passage of time would switch on a
bright tomorrow, where I would accomplish
all the great things I wanted to accomplish.
Then I would get to do it again the next day,
and the next, until I died a very old and very
content man.

Those days were long gone and gone
forever I'd figured. The depression rack had a
death tug on me and it wasn't about to let up
any slack. I'd been undergoing heavy doses of
interferon treatments for cancer for about

seven weeks, and the stuff was landing one rapid body blow after another. The things I had previously enjoyed like dating, books, funny movies, woodworking, and growing tomatoes felt stupid now. They served no purpose. And, of course, no one around me understood this amazing, ingenuous discovery I made about life being pointless, except me. This state of mind became the tragic universe every cell in my brain now inhabited.

Except for one cell.

This one, rebel brain cell just wouldn't wave the white flag of surrender. The damn thing refuted my insightful theory that life didn't matter, and insisted I eat something—a small saltine would do. So there I was, on that cold February night, trying to obey the mutineer cell. Why couldn't it just fall in like the rest of my cancer-riddled cells and surrender? No, not this cell. It had a mind of its own. It ordered me to fight.

I hadn't eaten anything of substance for weeks without vomiting. The interferon treatments had caused nausea and explosive anxiety. Mornings were the worst. I would get up and have nothing in me to vomit, yet I'd spend hours, my knees planted on cold bathroom floor tiles as I hunched over the toilet, gagging and spitting up air, so violently my stomach muscles felt ripped to shreds. Every time I tried to swallow and catch my breath, it triggered more gagging, spitting, and fruitless ghost vomiting. I couldn't even hold down water and had had to go to the hospital daily, for weeks, to get re-hydrated. The doctor prescribed numerous types of nausea medicine. I vomited them, and blamed myself for not being strong enough to hold anything, not even water, down.

Often, in the wee hours of those cold January and February mornings, desperate for a break in my routine, I would slip on a coat and go for a walk. It was always deathly quiet, until I paused under streetlights to gag, the wretched sound echoing and puffing through the frigid streets. Alone and miserable, I felt embarrassed and irrationally afraid my staid New England neighbors would call the cops, who'd see the withered man I'd become and cart me away in a straight jacket. I couldn't eat, so I'd walk, to reclaim one activity that approached ordinary life—or at least to keep from going crazy. Luckily, that damn remaining brain cell led the charge, made me get out of bed and hunt like a possessed savage for the long-lost, feel-good endorphins my addled brain required to keep fighting. Once home again, on that jet-black, freezing-cold February night, my one lonely, brave cell had insisted I eat that saltine.

Nothing—not buttered toast or bacon or a grilled steak—smelled good or tasted good, and I knew eating that saltine would only give my stomach something to vomit, but I also knew I had to eat to live—I knew because my strong-willed mother had often told me so. So I grabbed onto that saltine with both hands, like it was a Coast Guard line dropped from a helicopter into the ocean, fully realizing that eating it would mean a rough climb to safety.

I nibbled a corner and then washed the crumbs down with the slightest sip of water, hoping the water would wash it past what felt like a brick wall between my throat and my stomach.

Once the water and bits of saltine breached that first wall, I sat there determinedly nibbling and sipping until that little cracker met its ultimate demise. My opponent was down and not getting back up for a final throw. I didn't gain an ounce of weight or feel like I had a ration of spinach, but being able to eat the entire cracker signaled that I'd turned a corner, like the world does when it quietly, some unsuspecting day in March, ushers in the tiniest seedlings of spring.

The next day, I stepped it up a notch. I boiled one strand of spaghetti. Not only was it food, it was cooked food, and cooking it and eating it gave me a project. I nibbled it slowly and then went for my walk, gagging occasionally, but managing to keep the lone, long strand inside me. Best of all, the fear lessened that my neighbors would see or hear me and think I'd gone mad. I quickly moved on to two strands of spaghetti and dressed those up with a little olive oil and sea salt, which soon began to smell and taste good.

I cannot recall the exact day I stopped gagging and vomiting. It's not important now. For a year or so, however, I would wake up every morning with some primal fear that I would never be able to eat again and this fear would trigger nausea and episodes of anxiety—what the doctors called "anticipatory nausea." The doctors also told me that nausea is a defense designed to help us, which serves as a warning to protect our bodies against something bad inside that requires purging. My body had to purge itself of cancer, and the battle raged on, one saltine and one strand of spaghetti at a time.

Eventually the anticipatory nausea quietly slipped away and with it the anxiety and perhaps irrational fears that I would starve to death. Gone were the irrational notions that being sick somehow made me a bad person and an outcast. In the end, my fighting brain cell and I took everything that 800-pound saltine could dish out, and together, found a way to make peace with it.

***

FOUR

That Bottom Drawer on the Left

*Where the caravan is looking for
a fjord, the fool on foot has
crossed the river.*
–Persian Proverb

I honestly don't know why I opened

that bottom drawer on the left. Maybe

because I'd suddenly remembered that it was

stuck the last time I'd tried to open it, about

three years prior, and now I felt ready to take

it on again. Maybe a thought popped into my head that there might be something valuable in that drawer.

Because it was June and fairly hot and humid, I figured the cheap materials would've swollen in the humidity and I'd be tugging on that drawer handle like I'd been known to do, for days, with stubborn saplings invading my tomato garden, before realizing I could make short work of them with a shovel. But this time I didn't have to fight stubborn root systems; this time the drawer slid open without much of a fight, offering me a chance to explore the contents of the sawdust-covered, ancient office desk in my cellar wood shop.

It's important to note that this desk looked like one of those objects someone gave you twenty years prior, to save themselves a trip to the dump. You had no use for it, but you bulldozed some clutter aside to make room and agree to accept the "gift," confident someday you'd find an important use for this utterly useless object. Years passed and the useless object remained useless, forcing you to plan repeatedly to haul it off to the scrap heap. Suddenly I was curious about what useless objects I might have squirreled away in that useless drawer on the bottom left of this useless desk. If, indeed, I had anything at all hidden away.

There, at the bottom of the drawer, I found a pair of boxing gloves I had abandoned nearly a decade ago. They weren't the big fat kind boxers wear in a heavy-weight match, but the flat leather ones, resembling the woolen mittens our mothers and aunts used to make us as fast as we could lose them. These gloves were the kind boxers use to train on the heavy bag or speed bag. I'd bought them in February, 2006, in a desperate move to knock out the cancer "cure" blahs sapping my physical and emotional strength. I don't think I could over emphasize the important role these gloves played in getting me back on my feet during my first bout with cancer. And yet, I can honestly say that if I'd never opened that drawer, I probably never would have thought of those faithful gloves ever again. Somehow, they'd been completely swabbed from my memory drive.

As I sat there, however, feelings surfaced, mostly one of feeling like a brute for leaving my old sparring partners all alone in the basement, in that dark, corner drawer, to duke it out on their own. I was no better than one of those dingos (slackers, dimwits, impervious dodoheads) who roll up all the car windows when it's 200 degrees out, leaving poor Fido to pant it out in the family SUV while they run a "quick" errand. These gloves were in my corner when I needed a hand. I owed 'em big. And how did I repay them? By shoving them into a drawer for a decade, as if they were a couple of John Doe objects who held no meaning. They deserved better.

I wasn't a boxer and never had been. To be a boxer you actually had to step into a boxing ring with another human being and proceed to throw, and attempt to block, punches. And, moreover, endure a few hard punches. Boxers got knocked down and got back up again. Other than an occasional round of bare knuckle brawls with my older brothers while growing up, I'd never done that. I was just a guy who'd come up with a desperate plan to stay in the ring when cancer was knocking him out that cold February in 2006.

A few months prior to coming up with that plan and buying those gloves, I had been diagnosed with fourth-stage melanoma. A couple of weeks after finding a tumor in my groin, a surgeon removed it. A follow-up pet scan revealed an inability to find "clean margins," which the doctor described as "problematic." They couldn't tell how far the cancer had spread. "You just keep cutting till you get it all out, and I'll do the rest," I'd said. I'd pulled a weed or two in my day, so knew exactly what I was talking about—as if it were really that simple.

A few weeks after that, the good doctor removed more than a dozen problematic lymph nodes from my right leg. We let my ailing leg heal for about six weeks and then dragged it in for follow up treatment. In 2005, they treated my kind of cancer with a drug called interferon, in hopes massive doses of

this killer drug would boost your immunity

and hopefully increase the length of time

you'd spend in remission. Sounded like a good

plan especially when the doctor told me, there

was a greater than 50 percent chance the

cancer would be back in fewer than five years.

I welcomed thoughts that "greater than 50

percent" could be as high as 100 percent and

pushed aside thoughts that "fewer than five

years" could be as little as one day. I had

nothing to lose and potentially everything to

gain. I bought into the interferon insurance

plan, even dismissed the doctor's warning that

interferon often caused depression as existential poppycock—and chose to see it as "nonproblematic." When it came to facing this prospect in my typical strong-and-silent, stoic New Englander way, I foolishly ranked myself a heavy weight.

Round One. That December, I spent every weekday in Treatment Room A at St. Elizabeth's Hospital in Brighton, Massachusetts (the hospital where I was born), where what appeared to be kind nurses poured an unassuming, clear liquid, down a clear tube, through a plastic needle, shot through the port-a-catheter sewn into my

chest and into an artery leading to my heart.
That round of interferon was called the
induction phase. As predicated, I fought hard
to come through it like a champ. Chump
would be more accurate.

Round Two. In January I graduated to
self-treatment, which meant injecting myself
into my leg at home with a lower dose of
interferon. I lasted about three weeks before
the stuff sucker punched me. I couldn't eat. I
vomited everything I tried to consume,
including water. Without nourishment, I lost
thirty pounds. I had no strength, and hair fell
off by the bushel full. The interferon snuck up

on me under the cover of 10th-Century darkness and zombied all my brain's happy cells. Still, I drove my withered frame, in a state of complete vacancy, to the hospital every day to get hydrated and cheered on by nurses and little white pills I popped like Halloween candy. Looking at those sparring gloves brought all this back and wide-eyed me like a swift uppercut to the solar plexus.

During the month of February in Boston, everything is cold and dead and hard and the sun rises too late and sets too early. I clearly remember my doctor in the examination room, sitting on a little swivel stool, looking hard into my eyes. We were a few weeks into my unsolicited hunger strike. He pointed his right index finger at the floor and twirled it around in a circle. "It's like you're going down a whirlpool and the lower you go the faster and faster it goes, and the rotations get shorter and shorter. We don't want to reach a point where we can't reverse it." He sighed, "We have to stop the interferon or you'll die."

That roundhouse to the jaw didn't knock me out, it splashed over me like a bucket of ice-cold water from the corner man. The doctor and nurses couldn't do anything more for me. It was up to me. I had to get myself out of this depression maelstrom and fight to regain strength, and determination, and momentum. But the old "catch 22": I had no physical strength to nurture the mental and no mental strength to nurture the physical. I had no choice, however. I had to start somewhere.

Round Three. I joined my town's public gym, which was last updated after acquiring surplus equipment from the Roman Colosseum. The gym had an old, lumpy heavy weight bag, Ace-bandaged together with duct tape, making it look as if it were stepping into the fifteenth round with busted ribs. The gym smelled of rust, sweat, mildew, and the early 1970s. Civil War surgeons would have refused to operate there. Still, it was a place to go. A daily routine. A purpose. I belonged to something.

Only the word "pathetic" could describe my initial workouts. I could bench the barbell a few times. Curl some five pounders. Stretch. Walk, then eventually trot, on the treadmill. I felt like that proverbial 90-lb weakling featured on the back of comic books I used to laugh at. I could have sworn at one point I heard a couple of gym rats conspiring to dump sand on the gym floor just so they could kick it in my face. If they had done so, I couldn't have even thrown cotton balls back at them. Anyway, putting bullies in their place wasn't my present objective.

Round Four. I needed to purge the apathy demons out of me. Punching the hell out of that heavy bag would be a start. I drove to Sears and bought the cheapest pair of sparring gloves I could find. Among other things I was broke. Cancer can do that to you too, especially when you're self-employed. It doesn't sound like much now, but simply having a plan—to do something like buy sparring gloves on credit so I could go toe-to-toe with a smelly, tattered, heavy-weight bag that never did anything to me—was everything to me at the time. I came up with a plan and executed said plan. Those little black, lambskin gloves gave me something I never thought I would have again—the feeling of looking forward to something.

Each one of my pathetic workouts ended with me pounding the bag. That was my reward. I wouldn't allow myself to hit the bag until I finished my routine, which little by little found new additions—my reward getting pushed further and further down the line.

Round Five, Six, Seven, Eight, and Nine. I went to that gym and punched that bag for weeks and slowly my strength and adrenaline began to build, along with my ability to down small portions of food and keep down water. From my perspective, the fight dragged on and on, but at some point a small vigor became evident—even to me—and I donned those gloves more often, put more zip into my workouts. My moods improved, my overall health improved, and eventually I was declared "in remission" and was able to resume my somewhat normal life.

Obviously, at some point, I'd shoved those sparring-partner gloves into the desk drawer and moved on to "important" things.

As I held the gloves now just above that open drawer, I actually chuckled. At the time of sparring, I imagined that I was putting that old bag into its place, but the gloves I presently held indicated otherwise. They looked brand new. The painted lambskin still sported its black sheen. They were as flat and stiff as slate never having taken on that grip shape well-worn leather gloves earn from true wear and tear and sweat. I guess my haymakers and upper cuts weren't as deadly as old Killer here thought.

But like I said, I'm no fighter.

In fact, I came to the quick realization

that I would never use the gloves again. I

didn't even try them on for old time's sake

before tossing them onto the passenger's seat

of my car with big plans to give them to my

nephew Liam. Three months later, the gloves

had gotten no farther than the passenger's

side floor mat. Every now and then, from the

corner of my eye, I catch them coming at me.

Or maybe it's me coming for them. These

transitional objects can be difficult to

transition from, even long after we think

they're dead and buried in the dark drawers of nowhere. I just didn't need them anymore to go the distance.

Round Fifteen. Someday soon I'll make sure the gloves find their way to Liam. He's a good student and a humble athlete. Not afraid to get his hands dirty. The kind of kid you really root for. The kind you hope slides open an old drawer some day and finds a bit of treasure.

***

FIVE

The Old Man and the Mutt

You will find adventure on the road
not in the Inn.
—Cervantes

I sometimes get the feeling my right leg

is dying on me. Maybe that's an unfair

accusation. My leg's been good to me and is

owed better. Perhaps it's me dying on my leg.

My leg and I's odyssey began September 27, 2005, when a fight to beat cancer meant a right groin dissection, which left a scar running from my inner thigh to my right pelvis. During my follow-up appointment, a few weeks after the surgery, my surgeon inspected the wound—that's what the doctors called it, as if I got hit on D-Day or something—and shook his head in amazement at the lack of swelling.

He smiled as he made fists, holding them parallel to his chest, the knuckles butting each other and the backs of his hands facing me. "I remember," he said, as he pulled his fists apart, looking like Clark Kent ripping his button-down shirt off his chest, "I really had you opened up." We had a good relationship and could talk to each other like that. "You did well," he said, admiring how much the swelling had gone down. Yeah, like I really had anything to do with it.

Post-op I had kept my leg and hip elevated on pillows, walked and wiggled my toes a lot to keep the circulation going. I'd also spent hours each day massaging my leg muscles, as if reshaping a large block of clay.

I'd also started walking right after the operation. Two days post-op I promised a nurse that I'd go to the bathroom like a big boy, if they would only pull the tube out of my urinary tract. I didn't know anything could be shoved into that tender spot, especially such a fat tube. Tube free, I sneaked off my hospital floor and took the elevator down three flights to visit my eighty-nine year old aunt Alice, who had been admitted to treat her annual pneumonia.

The second she saw me ambling through her door, her eyes lit up—with fury. "What are you doing here? Get back to bed." Then frowning, "Do your doctors know what you're up to?" They did not, and dear old

Aunt Alice would have ratted me out in two shakes of a lamb's tail. Me and my leg hotfooted it out of there—actually, hobblefooted would be more accurate— achieving a clean get away. If she could get all fired up and bark out orders, all was fine on the Alice front.

When I left the hospital three days after my surgery, I felt like a shark that would die if he stopped swimming and convinced myself that if I kept walking, I could outrun the cancer. Still, I needed more inspiration than mimicking a shark's lust for life—luckily I had something more inspiring at home than sharks—magnificent creatures that they are.

Ten years earlier I paid the local pound $75.00 for a four-year-old, three-legged dog named Shadow—long before people rescued dogs and tied the "rescued" tale to the purchase. Shadow's entire right foreleg had been amputated, but she seemed blissfully unaware of this fact. She chased squirrels, stole street hockey balls from important tie-breaking games, and could jump into the back of my Ford F-150 pick-up truck when she heard my keys jingling. When I first bought Shadow, my brother Jay and I owned a full-service landscaping business. Shadow went everywhere with us.

Above all, Shadow loved the ocean. Any body of water really. I had no idea Shadow could swim, until I drove her to the beach on our second day together and, once unleashed, she shot off like a cannon ball. Jumping. Diving. Splashing. Swimming the Atlantic surf. Half lab and all heart, Shadow swam farther and farther out, doggedly chasing some sea gulls bobbing up and down in the water ahead of her. Like Popeye, she was who she was. One less leg didn't change that. My guiding inspiration sadly swam her last sea gull hunt long ago, but after my surgery, she sure

showed me how to get back into the swim.
Shadow was there for me in a way no one else
could be, and even now she's with me every
step of the way.

Once home from the hospital post-
surgery, Shadow and I began my walking
regimen "day one." In my pajamas and
slippers, I (we) walked from the telephone
pole located at the corner of my driveway to
the next one up a somewhat manageable hill
and back. Soon I was successfully walking
around the block; before long, Lexington
center became my newfound marker. While
walking, cognizance of the still visible wound

would start me worrying that I would spilt open like a watermelon tossed out of a getaway car, if I fell down. Then, I'd look at old faithful Shadow po-going along beside me and suddenly the fear would subside and I'd keep trudging along. Within three weeks I was sufficiently ambulatory to resume teaching my night course in detective fiction at Boston College.

Three months later, at another follow-up with my surgeon, he was again surprised—and impressed—that I'd somehow staved off whatever swelling one would expect. With so many lymph nodes removed, the body's circulation is typically shot—unable to process many fluids. The good doctor expected my leg to be swollen like a water balloon—and that that level of swelling would become chronic. Prior to surgery, I'd worried that I'd never be able to work outside again, doing things I enjoyed like mowing my lawn, pushing a shovel into my tomato garden, or riding my bike. Thanks to Shadow, I had walked away the usual side effects and was given clearance to do all those things and things I'd only dreamed of doing like landscaping, running, and darting around town on my old Ross ten-speed.

Approximately two years after my operation, I felt so alive and vital, I joined the National Guard. I was forty. But my leg felt fantastic, and we wanted to serve. We were convinced we could do it, and on March 13, 2008, we raised our right arm and took the oath to serve. On September 17, 2008—almost three years to the day of my operation—my leg and I found ourselves on a plane flying to Fort Jackson, South Carolina, for Basic Army Combat Training. We were both forty-one by that time.

For ten weeks my leg and I ran, jumped, climbed, rappelled walls, made up the top bunk with hospital corners. One night, we crawled under barbed wire, through sand and mud, as live rounds whizzed over our head. We had the time of our lives, and passed every physical training test. For a couple of old soldiers, we even nailed our last basic training run—two miles in fourteen minutes and thirty-six seconds. In 2011-2012, holding the rank of sergeant, we did an eleven-month tour in Afghanistan, which involved jumping onto whirly birds and humping body armor, ammo, and assault packs. My right leg took me places I never would have gone had I never faced that surgery and the recovery it required. My right leg owes me nothing and I have no right to put in for any rebates—but that doesn't stop me from worrying about it daily.

Lately, it's been dragging a bit. It's my fault. My leg was born to hoof. My Army days are kaput. Now I make a living pushing paper across a desk. Sitting most of the day in a chair cuts off my leg's circulation and causes it to fall asleep. It's starting to realize that it's missing most of its lymph nodes, creating strange pains in my thigh and muscle tightening in my calf. My right foot grows cold as winter slate, and other times it feels like there's a swarm of bees buzzing around in there.

Even as I write now, the numbness and swelling in my leg, and an annoying pain now radiating in my right hip, remind me that my leg doesn't want to sit this day out with the slackers. My leg is coming at me like Shadow with a ball in her mouth, whipping her tail telling me, It's time for a swim, old man. Get up and play. Daylight's burning.

Alas, I have bills to pay, plus taxes and hidden fees that require my attention—the usual adult responsibilities that a leg couldn't possibly understand. Like Shadow, I soldier on, doing my best to ignore my throbbing leg.

Still, I sometimes wonder whether it's better to be carried off in one big gale or little by little, by a series of gentle sea breezes, to be distracted by the sun as the tide goes out inch by inch. Will I join the ranks of those caught dozing in a beach chair only to wake up and wonder where it all went? Or will I join the hardy souls swimming with the sharks, navigating swift currents, defeating whatever man-eaters lurk below, and crashing joyfully onshore with the waves?

I don't think I've figured out yet whether my leg, in its present condition, is the receding tide or an invitation to face the big

gale head on. Deep down—I know. Come

hell or high water, we're going up or down

together. In the end, like my trusty friend

Shadow, neither my right leg, nor I, has any

intention of sitting this one out.

***

SIX

Move Over, the Cheeseburger's Driving

A bit of fragrance always clings to the hand
that gives you roses.
–Old Chinese proverb

I would do all the driving.

The idea popped into my mind one day in

March 2006, when cancer cures had left me

physically weak, unable to eat, and feeling like

a man without purpose. But not anymore. My Aunt Alice, in her ninetieth year, had just been diagnosed with a skin cancer that was feverishly devouring her chin. She couldn't drive, so I offered to take her back and forth to her radiation treatments, grateful that she needed my help.

Aunt Alice was just a few months shy of her ninetieth birthday, but her mind was still sharp as a carpet knife. She was ambulatory, but bad knees from a lifetime of hard work and adventurous play, usually reserved for the men of her generation, had caught up with her.

Alice had worked as a bank teller her entire career and had taken care of her parents in their golden years, seeing her mother through a horrific battle with Lou Gehrig's disease and her father through a long battle with "senility," what dementia or Alzheimer's disease was called back in the day of Sunday suppers and family prayer. Regardless of its medical name, diagnosis, or prognosis, my grandfather had slipped into the late stages at a time when only the Alices of the world took care of someone with his needs at home.

At the time, Alice had lived her entire life in the house she was born into in 1916.

She'd never married, choosing instead to live a rooted, yet adventurous life. As far back as the Great Depression she worked hard as a bank teller at the friendly neighborhood bank during the week. For many, she was the friendly neighborhood bank. As kids, it was always a special treat when our mother swung Alice's 1963 Bel Air (my mother often borrowed her car) through the bank's drive-through when Alice was "manning" the window. From our viewpoint, Aunt Alice pushed some secret button, releasing a metal draw that magically pushed through the brick wall, revealing bank giveaway swag, like balloons or pens or items kids coveted but had no use for, like cheap sponges inked with the bank's name. Without a doubt, Alice was the most important banker we knew.

On weekends, Alice would go on trips with her female friends, skiing the slopes of Vermont and New Hampshire. She also loved ice skating on nearby ponds, hiking throughout Western Massachusetts, and swimming and diving on Cape Cod. As a young woman, she would walk to work in order to save the trolley fare for her adventures. During WWII, however, she donated any money she saved to the war effort.

You'd also find Alice cleaning the gutters on her three-story house and scraping, sanding, and applying polyurethane to its hardwood floors. She'd also paint, clip the hedges, shovel snow, knit, and bake, as well as hunt down and scour sporting goods stores where she could buy baseball gloves and Bobby Orr hockey and Carl "Yaz" Yazstremski shirts for her nephews.

I'd found her one winter afternoon, when she was in her mid-eighties (her lap buried in yarn), looking forlorn. "What's wrong? I'd asked, fearing something medical might be wrong.

"I don't think I can shovel my roof anymore," she said, pointing to the sun-porch's flat roof. Unbeknownst to the family, Aunt Alice would climb out the window after a nor'easter and clear mounds of snow off the roof.

One of Aunt Alice's specialties was knitting mittens and hats for her gaggle of nieces and nephews. We would, of course, lose them every year, or at least half of them. I spent many a winter with mismatched mittens, as did my brothers. I can still smell those wool mittens drying off on the cast-iron radiators in my parent's farmhouse.

Aunt Alice would also organize and run church bazaars and knit sweaters and blankets to sell on the cheap—probably for far less than she paid for the yarn—to raise money for "this or that" parish need. In her lifetime, she made—at her own expense—thousands of baptismal bibs for the neighboring, Saint John's Church.

At the time, street parking was always impossible in Aunt Alice's North Cambridge neighborhood, so people would regularly park in Saint John's lot. Eventually, the church issued a "No Parking - Tow Away" policy.

But, if anyone in our family parked there and wrote a note saying "Visiting Alice" and tossed it on the dashboard, we were never ticketed or towed.

Aunt Alice was also active and community conscious in summer. Sometimes we'd find her on her hands and knees, working her way up and down the brick sidewalks, using a butter knife to pry loose weeds that she'd then compost. She'd even keep at it until she rid hers and the neighbors' sidewalks of those pesky weeds.

Well into her eighties you'd see Aunt Alice pulling her laundry cart through the streets of North Cambridge. She had a washing machine and dryer at home, but the water meter was connected to her tenants' (two nuns) water meter and she refused to add costs to their water bill.

But now, after a lifetime of doggedly taking care of herself and many others, once cancer attacked her chin, Aunt Alice finally welcomed a hand. Although it had advanced so quickly it looked like she had an open gunshot wound on the right side of her chin, the oncologist said it was localized and would likely respond well to radiation.

Secretly, I think Alice enjoyed our daily

trips for the radiation treatments. I know I did. Once we were "out and about," she'd coax me into running little errands, picking up "this or that" she needed at home, like tea, stationery, stamps, and many things I felt sure she really didn't need.

About halfway through her treatments, Alice began asking if I wanted to have a quick bite to eat somewhere. Despite having very little appetite and being constantly nauseous—unable to hold down little more than a few saltines at a time—I always said yes, because she wanted to go. Sometimes I'd reluctantly eat a few morsels and, if it was bland enough, could sometimes hold it down a little longer.

On our last radiation-day adventure, we decided to visit my parents' gravesite at North Cambridge's Catholic Cemetery. It was one of those mercurial March days in New England, when occasional spangles of sun pierced the chill, grey sky. If you walked into the sunlight at just the right angle, you'd get a splash of warmth, a spilt-second reminder that spring would soon, once again, eclipse winter. Then, seconds later, frigid gusts of wind would remind you that it wasn't time to pull out the swim trunks.

Despite feeling physically frail, self-absorbed, and an emotional wreck, I worried about Aunt Alice navigating the frozen grass and frost heaves that made the walk to my parents' gravesite perilous for us both. She'd metaphorically held my hand through many dark days, so imagine my surprise, when the second I clasped her hand, I felt a bolt of warmth spread throughout my body. Just like the sunlight brightened the grey skies, Aunt Alice's warmth suffused me with feelings of peace and calm and purpose, feelings my cancer and interferon treatments had convinced me might be gone for good.

Within seconds, I also felt an indescribable surge of power, as if Aunt Alice had deliberately transferred all the fight she no longer needed to me. Whatever nerves and nausea I'd been feeling up to that moment completely dissipated, and I felt something I'd not felt for months—hunger.

After offering prayers at my parents' gravesite, Aunt Alice suggested we have lunch at Brigham's, her favorite joint, where I eagerly downed a cheeseburger and fries. It had been months since I enjoyed food, particularly a cheeseburger, as much as I did that day. I knew I wasn't out of the cancer woods yet, and indeed more difficult days lay ahead, but at least that day I eagerly devoured some of my favorite food, reassuring myself that strength and vigor would return. As it turned out, all I had to do to make it happen was hold out my hand.

Alice passed not long after, at age ninety-one, and we buried her with her parents, in the family plots near where we'd prayed together that chilly March afternoon. Even though I lived nearby and could easily indulge in regular moping sessions by her gravesite, I knew she'd want none of that. She'd want me to keep fighting, stay focused on the positive, and do what I have to do to heal and get stronger without a lot of complaining, so that's what I did.

I sometimes wondered, however, if she knew that I got what I needed from her the moment we clasped hands that day, that her lifelong determination to fight whatever battles had to be won had given me my life back. Then I'll laugh, confident that Aunt Alice would think I'm foolish for believing at the time that I was helping her. She'd been driving all along.

***

SEVEN

All That Matters

You are not what you think you are;
but what you think, you are.
—Norman Vincent Peale

I'm not sure I understood why at the

time, but the thought of having radical surgery

in 2014 to remove my second malignant

tumor in nine years didn't worry me. When

making the decision to operate, I'd joked with

the surgeon that I had the easy part. All I had to do was sleep through it while he'd be on his feet all day. "I'll be out the entire time and if I pass, I won't feel a thing," I said, "and that's all that matters."

Over the preceding year, two cancer specialists (including the one who saved my life in 2005) and two surgeons (including the one who also saved my life in 2005) told me that the tumor was inoperable, even after using chemotherapy to shrink the tumor. And the doctor who finally agreed to operate on me had wanted the tumor to shrink more, but, as predicted, when the chemo stopped working, the tumor stopped shrinking. He scheduled the surgery because I had no other viable choice. My chances of living much longer, with the tumor or with surgery, were somewhere between a crap shot and a Hail Mary pass thrown by a Satanic worshiper. Still, I just went about my business going to work every day and squaring away my everyday household chores, as if the big day would come and go like any other. It would. Life would go on with or without my heart beating.

I worked until the last moment, allocating Saturday through Wednesday to get in order what I had to. One of the things I wanted to do was spend as much time with my oldest brother Jay as I could. The Monday before surgery we decided to drive up to Salem, Massachusetts to visit the gravesite of a Civil War United States Marine Corporal named Austin Quinby. Quinby served aboard the U.S.S. *Kearsarge* during the Civil War, along with our great-grandfather John J. McAleer, a Marine private. On June 19, 1864, off the coast of Cherbourg, France, the *Kearsarge*, consisting largely of a New England crew, defeated the Confederate's most successful raider, the C.S.S. *Alabama*. Under the deft command of Raphael Semmes, the *Alabama* had all but wiped out North Atlantic commerce during the latter part of the Civil War by sinking or capturing nearly seventy ships. We knew this because, upon my return from Afghanistan, Jay and I began bestowing order to our great-grandfather's Civil War artifacts, as well as the extensive library our father (his grandson) preserved. In doing so, we'd opened up a fascinating world initially based on the bits and pieces Dad and my Uncle Robert shared with us through the years.

As we held actual artifacts from the

ship, sorted through the old photographs of the *Kearsarge*'s crew, and researched more about the ship and its thirty-four month Civil War cruise, we became increasingly fascinated with its history. The photographs we had were primarily of the surviving crewmembers, taken during annual gatherings, years after the battle. We watched them age and disappear as documented by each annual dinner's photographs and an actual ledger keeping minutes of the gatherings. Our own great-grandfather's final attendance occurred in 1915. Still, the remaining crew kept up the annual tradition until the mid-1920s, doing their best to keep their service and memory of their beloved ship alive.

As we began to identify the old men in the photos, we started calling them by name when we discussed the history we were uncovering. We had heard our father mention some of these names, but they'd just been names at the time. Now they had faces and bodies and smiles and comradeship associated with their names. As we learned of their brave deeds and sacrifices, they were no longer black and white—they were flesh and blood.

Because I loved delving into history, these men soon consumed me. Day after day,

as I read old newspaper clippings, a copy of
the ships journal kept by Quinby, and other
books on the subject, once owned and held by
our great-grandfather—a couple of them even
signed by him—the crew of the *Kearsarge*
carried my soul away to one 19th-century
adventure after another—far away from
cancer land.

One day, Jay and I found an August 18,
1897 handwritten letter from Quinby
addressed to our great-grandfather. (It has
since been donated to the Peabody Essex
Museum.) The letter contained Quinby's
home address in Salem. When we discovered

he was buried in Salem, we decided to pay him a visit on Monday, April 7th, coincidentally the anniversary of Quinby's death, on April 7, 1922. We soon found his grave and offered our respects. Etched on the back of his gravestone is the image of the *Kearsarge* and the date of its battle with the *Alabama*. As we learned, fifty-eight years after the battle, Quinby, with one final proud trim of her sails, retired to the bottom deck of his beloved ship for the last time. The helm was now in our hands Jay and I reckoned.

We then visited Quinby's home and took pictures to add to our library. Afterward we had a peaceful lunch at a restaurant

overlooking Salem harbor. We felt proud that

we'd come to see a grave and an old house

that apparently few knew about or visited.

Quinby's house was not a national landmark,

like the White House or Monticello. His was

merely home to a patriot who, by all accounts,

lived a good, simple life and served his

country honorably. Quinby had been a man,

once young and full of adventure and justice,

who'd been willing to put it all on the line for

the ultimate cause of freedom; a man credited

with firing the first shot and the last shot that

sank the *Alabama*; a man now virtually

forgotten by history. Perhaps it was strange that, in the few hours before my surgery, I would spend it visiting Quinby's house and grave, but it was a welcome distraction, and I felt a sense of contentment for doing so. Besides, I was with my big brother.

My brother Jay, like our great-grandfather, is also a Marine. Jay would be driving me to the hospital for my surgery three days later. It may seem like a little thing, but knowing you have a reliable mate to get you to the hospital is a huge relief. I'd learned this when I became friendly with a woman after my first battle with cancer. She had fourth-stage breast cancer and when she had to go to the hospital for a double mastectomy, her live-in boyfriend—living in her house—claimed to have something more important to do. She'd had to take the subway alone to the hospital. At the time we met, she was still with him, still defending him. The last time we had dinner together, however, she was happy, smiling and joking, still teaching and enjoying time with her girlfriends on Cape Cod. She had finally cut her anchor loose and got back on course. She's gone now, but I often think of her when I have a battle to face, grateful that I have a true mate, like my brother Jay to man the decks. In fact, during my first battle with cancer, Jay would often work double shifts as an EMT in order to keep the wolf off our door.

I could always rely on Jay to be ready on time and I didn't have to worry about him navigating the streets from our house to the hospital. As an EMT (whose duties often included being at the ready at Fenway Park) and a swap driver for a major car manufacturer, Jay has driven and ploughed through every freeway, back street, local road, cut-through, and alley Boston and its surrounding suburbs could dish out, in any kind of weather, any time of day and night.

Moreover, Boston is notorious for it's

incomprehensible tangle of streets and a

noticeable lack of signage.

Whenever I, or anyone else, asked Jay

for directions, he'd come up with at least a

dozen different routes of how to get to the

destination. Then, he'd produce a handy

timetable chart and map out the most

advantageous times to take said routes. He'd

also insist on a thorough vehicle safety

inspection, which would invariably result in a

quick tire rotation and belt and fluid

inspection. Then, he'd send you on your way,

but only after you repeated the directions he'd just provided, word for word.

Jay also operated on Marine time. If he said, "Let's leave at 7 a.m. to avoid traffic," this really meant he'd be at your door anxious to depart at 6:30 a.m. And, since Marines hold that if you are not fifteen minutes early, then you are fifteen minutes late, then 6:30 a.m. really meant 6:15 a.m. The bottom line, I had no one else to blame on surgery day when Jay drug me out of the house forty-five minutes ahead of schedule.

Within minutes, we entered the confines of Boston, arcing over the

Longfellow Bridge, passing the Charles Street Subway Station, eyeballing our destination, Massachusetts General Hospital (known locally as "MGH"), on our immediate left. I happened to look to my right and noticed West Cedar Street. "Hey," I said, "that's the street where Dr. Dixwell lived! Let's take a look, we have plenty of time."

Doctor John Dixwell was another interesting person we'd come to know from identifying crewmembers of the *Kearsarge*. I often heard my father mention his name when regaling us with tales of our great-grandfather serving on the deck of the *Kearsarge* while the canons were blazing. A little digging revealed that he was a graduate of the Boston Latin School, Harvard University, and Harvard Medical School, and, the brother-in-law of Oliver Wendell Holmes. I even found a picture of Dixwell from the 1930s. There he was standing outside Harvard University. He wore a broad-rimmed hat. Its rim shaded a stern face, which contradicted his kind, hooded eyes. He sported a thick, white sawhorse mustache, and a long, leather coat sporting oversized buttons. His face seemed weathered and sad, as if he were a Civil War general tired of sending his boys off to their death.

As a famous Boston surgeon, Dixwell donated much of his time to taking care of Civil War survivors as the surgeon for the Kearsarge Association of Naval Veterans, my great-grandfather among the veterans he cared for. As the survivors of the *Kearsarge* grew older and older and fewer and fewer, we learned that Dixwell would drive the sailors back and forth to their annual reunions. He later served as president of their survivors' association and, from what we could discern, did his best to keep their spirits alive, as a thank you for their service. Dixwell had no children, which may be why his own spirit and

good deeds were all but forgotten—but not

by Jay and I, not even on the day I was facing

life or death surgery. On that day and many

others, I welcomed Jay's willingness to whirl

through the eddies of time with me, and our

ancestors, once more.

Wordlessly, Jay made a few artful cuts

and quickly wended us to our new destination.

Dixwell's brownstone on West Cedar Street in

Boston Proper was as we expected: a sturdy,

somewhat majestic brick structure, with

granite steps, and a wrought-iron railing. Like

Quinby's home, it wasn't designated a

museum and there was no one there to offer any fanfare. No brass band there to greet us. We simply looked at his home for a few moments and drove off to the inevitable.

At Mass General it dawned on Jay and I for the first time that Dixwell may have been a Mass General surgeon. After all, he lived within walking distance and the hospital was founded in 1811. Had his good will over the years helped, even perhaps in the smallest way, create a tradition of attracting the world's most renowned surgeons to Mass General— including the one who would save my life? Maybe it was all of the research into the brave men of the *Kearsarge* that infused me with an indefatigable fighting spirit that morning, or maybe it was simply imagining that a man like Dixwell may have walked these same halls, successfully saving lives a century ago. I liked believing that Dixwell's goodwill still made the rounds at Mass General after all these years and that somehow his spirit could play a role in my successful surgery. I know for some it's probably a whole bunch of horsepucky, but these men had become so real to me I found it plausible he might really be there in spirit, watching over me along with my brothers Jay and Paul, both there in living color. Good deeds have no expiration date.

As the hospital crew rolled me into that operating room, I could feel the blessings and strength that came from knowing that men like Dixwell and Quinby and my great-grandfather once walked this earth, and so could my big brother in exploration, Jay.

Turns out that's all that mattered.

***

EIGHT

Who Would Have Known Those Were Good Times?

Absence of occupation is not rest. A mind quite vacant is a man distressed.
–William Cowper

The only thing longer than hospital days are hospital nights—especially when you're not sleeping through them. That first night, after my groin dissection surgery in

2005 to remove cancer from my leg, I'd shut my eyes and swear I drifted off for hours; then I'd wake, focus my eyes, and see the clock had moved only fifteen, short minutes. Then I'd see my older brother, Paul, from the corner of my right eye, half awake himself, squirming in an apparent effort to fit his six-foot-five, 220-pound frame into a hard, undersized, and unyielding chair beside my bed.

Paul's night had begun badly. We'd both been told by the doctors that the plan was to manage pain levels by starting a morphine drip once I got to my room. When that didn't happen, my exasperated brother inquired at the nurses' station. A nonplussed nurse explained that there had been a mix up; somehow no one Faxed a prescription to the pharmacy, which was now closed. I always thought hospitals just magically had post-operative drugs at the ready. I didn't realize "someone" had to Fax pharmacies. Anyway, that was the party line and though it irked Paul, who could have just as easily flung some of those nurses out the window, he returned to me and delivered the news, fuming. Luckily for them, whatever pain drugs they'd given me for the surgery had not yet dissipated, so I was able to talk Paul down.

Once my brother saw that I was awake, rather than complain, he'd ask if I needed anything. Water? A pillow? Beat up the innocent hospital staff member who just came on shift, but could readily be blamed for the hospital not having the right pain meds on order? I imagine it wasn't easy for Paul to fidget in that awful chair all night, but he stuck it out, as so many loved ones do. I don't imagine he was the first one to turn that chair into a makeshift campsite.

Perhaps it was the meds—or rather the lack of sufficient meds—that convinced me hospital execs hire evil pencil pushers, all of whom charge exorbitant fees to conduct studies on how to dissuade visiting friends and family from keeping an eye on things. They likely invented that torturous visitors' chair—modeled after Salem witch-trial racks, or a Catherine's wheel—for the sick purpose of limiting the number of visitors, all so it would be easier for them to sweep under a hospital bed. In all honesty, as a former nursing home custodian, I wasn't entirely opposed to the scheme. Nevertheless, that first post-surgery night, when the proper doses of meds had been mismanaged, it was a long night. Alternating watches, Paul and I managed to push through.

Two months later, when I began interferon treatments, Paul took a week off from work and daily drove me back and forth to the hospital. About an hour after taking interferon, muscle pain invades your whole body, much like the flu does. You feel raw and mortal and cold; and, almost as suddenly, you feel like your body has gone up in flames. I would arrive home feeling like every square inch of my body had been pounded with a meat tenderizer. We'd get home around 2:30 in the afternoon, and I'd go straight to bed.

Paul would throw a few blankets on the floor beside my bed and keep watch. We spent that entire week watching movies, talking about the good old days, and joking about things only he and I would understand. Even if I told him I'd be okay for a few hours, he refused to leave my side.

Paul and I have always been close. Our family has an unusual generational breakdown. The first four children were baby boomers and Paul and I were latchkey kids. My mother was around for the first fours' early child rearing, but Paul and I were cut loose from the apron strings much earlier.

Paul is two years older and our mother went back to work around the time I started school, leaving Paul and I to choose our outfits, cook our breakfast, find our way to school, forage for food after school, do our laundry, and manufacture money-making schemes. We became de facto partners.

There was many-a-morning we would pull kitchen chairs up to the stove, retrieve our great-grandmother's frying pan (which we still use) and fry up some eggs. One morning, I couldn't have been older than six, we talked about opening a restaurant together "when we grew up to be grown-up men." From that point forward it seems, self-reliance ruled the day and, for this, I eternally thank our parents.

We were unleashed from grammar school by 12:15 p.m. every Thursday, whereupon Paul and I would raid Mrs. Dentler's rhubarb garden, Mr. Connolly's apple tree, or look for lost change around parking meters to buy "sensible lunches," like candy bars, potato chips, and baseball cards. We also checked phone booths for forgotten change. There was no better feeling than sticking your finger into the chrome change slot and feeling that lucky nickel, dime or quarter slide around the stainless steel coin bucket. Paul and I always split the spoils, right down the middle.

Sometimes we'd find some lucky kid whose mother "didn't have to work" and we'd get ourselves invited to lunch. It sounds surreal now, but times were different then. Many of our classmates were in the same boat. At the time, it seemed like those afternoons were endless, but, in reality, our mother would arrive home by 2:30 p.m. to let us into the house, making us latchkey kids without the key—because she was afraid we'd get into mischief inside the house. If she ran late, a convenient tree (we named the Tom

Sawyer tree) and a loose second-story window solved our problem. We'd raid sleeves of saltines or graham crackers, just enough to fill our bellies, but not so much mom would know something was missing. If she only knew, we'd snicker . . . but I'm confident now she knew all along.

As we got older, we formed lawn-mowing, leaf-raking, and snow-shoveling partnerships, always splitting everything fifty-fifty and never arguing over a dime. We even saved a dime or two along the way. This created a lifetime pattern of working hard and saving, which allowed us to buy the family cottage, along with our brother Jay, after our parents passed.

The summer after my first surgery and interferon debacle, while I was still worrying about whether the cancer was truly gone for good, I decided to build a backyard patio at the cottage. I wanted to make it solely from bricks found washed up from the sea. Paul and I called them sea bricks because, much like sea glass, the battering sand and surf leaves them looking worn and smoothed and breaks them up into different shapes and sizes. Most of the bricks come from old lobster traps and ship ballasts. One would think sea bricks would be a rare commodity, but you can find a fair amount of them if you look, and your booty exponentially increases when you have a search partner.

The patio I had in mind would be only about seven feet by seven feet. As I broke ground, my neighbors looked at me like I'd lost my mind. But not Paul. For him, building a patio out of sea bricks seemed the most natural thing—at least that he and I would do anyway. He began joining me in my walks on the beach, combing for bricks. I knew that he recognized how helpful it was for me to have a project and complete it, so once we exhausted our own beach, we spent the summer driving around to other beaches, greedily hauling in every sea brick we could scavenge. Soon, the neighbors, who admitted that they'd once feared I'd become the village nutcase, were now actively invested in my success. They would periodically pop by to check on the progress and, each time I visited the beach, would expect full reports from me as to when it would be completed. Many neighbors, including the neighborhood kids (one of whom was fighting a rare cancer herself), joined in on the sea brick hunt.

By late August the patio still needed a

few more square feet of sea bricks, however, it looked beautiful. The different shapes and sizes and colors all seemed to marry each other perfectly, as if the sea herself had envisioned my little patio all along. Each brick manufacturer has its own way of making bricks, so those sea bricks had a charming lack of uniformity that created a unique mosaic. As Paul and I gathered even more bricks, I began to believe that I would have it completed by Labor Day, as per my make-shift plan.

Then one late August morning I woke up blindsided by a debilitating depression. Though I'd been putting up a good front, I still suffered from nausea and constantly

worried that I would suddenly lose my ability

to eat. As I lay in bed, lethargic and lifeless,

unable to think of any reason why I should

get up, I suddenly heard the familiar, chalky

tumble of sea bricks softly landing on the

ground beneath my bedroom window. Paul

had been combing the beach early that

morning for bricks, and his enthusiasm was all

I needed to climb out of bed. A half hour

later, we had his morning catch installed.

When Labor Day came around, we knocked

in the final bricks. The satisfaction of

gathering all those sea bricks and creating

something together was all we needed—and I
needed—to feel a real sense of
accomplishment.

These days, the patio has weeds
growing though its joints, but those weeds
kind of hold things together—and make it
look like it's always been there. Paul and I like
to place two comfortable Adirondack chairs
on our patio and sit facing the ocean, soaking
up the morning sun. On rare occasions—not
as many as we envisioned when building the
patio—we drink home-brewed coffee made
from our mother's vintage, six-cup corning
ware percolator and eat bagels slathered with

homemade wild beach-plum jelly we make every August, thanks to a tradition started by our father, while catching up on the good old days. On these occasions we make plans for the good old days to come. We rest our mugs on a table I made from three lobster pot buoys and a couple of slabs of driftwood, another project that had the neighbors looking at me crosswise.

It's funny how time smoothes out the edges. Just like the ocean smoothes whatever falls within its wake. I don't dwell on the way I felt lying in that hospital bed, or the flu-like symptoms and endless nights devoured by the world's worst case of depression ever recorded—by me. What I do remember is the comfort of having my brother Paul by my side.

Have I lost my marbles for recalling that first week of interferon treatments with Paul as if it were some kind of cub scout camping trip? Or for wishing we had another patio project to work on so I could find the meaning and purpose of life? To beat back the apathy demons? I must've lost my mind. When I think about Paul pulling the all-nighter in the hospital chair, sleeping on the floor all week, and putting aside his own responsibilities to search for sea bricks and build a patio to keep me from drifting in a sea of despair, it all seems absurd. I couldn't possibly ask him to re-create those back-breaking nights and worry-ridden days, simply because the memories of him being by my side fosters a longing for "the good old days."

But here's the thing about Paul: I never asked him the first time.

**

NINE

Robin Company Soldiers On

Good books, like good friends,
are few and chosen;
the more select, the more enjoyable.
–Louisa May Alcott

At the age of forty I was seriously

considering joining the Massachusetts Army

National Guard. In addition to wanting to

blow out all the cobwebs from what I had

been through—with battling my own cancer,

and the care taking and ultimate loss of both

of my parents within days of each other—

many of the people I admired most in my life

had served in the military. My father, my

Uncles: Robert, Buddy, Gunter, Joe, my

brother Jay, and my friends Lenny and Robin

had all served.

Throughout my high school and college

years, I worked as a custodian at a local

nursing home. My bosses and supervisors

were all World War II or Korean War

veterans. During my rite-of-passage years,

they taught me how to buff, wax, and strip

floors, fix toilets, and play cribbage. They also taught me how to make elderly women, long forgotten by family members, smile and feel special again. They taught me how to listen with sincerity as withering men—literally from the Victorian era—griped about taxes, failed prostates, and how nothing was like it used to be.

The veterans who taught me how to swing a hammer, listening to others, and the importance of punching in on time were mostly gone by the time I turned forty, which made my friendship with Robin Moore all the more special. Robin had survived World War

II (where he served under the command of Jimmy Stewart), Viet Nam, the streets of New York, and, among other things, a bounty put out on him by Fidel Castro. In addition to being the author nearly 100 books, including *The Green Berets*, *The French Connection*, and *The Hunt for Bin Laden*, to me, Robin was most of all a dear friend after my parents died.

We began an unlikely friendship when I mailed him a letter in the spring of 2001 asking him a few questions about the author James M. Cain, for a book my father was working on at the time structured around his own interviews with Cain. I would have done backward summersaults upon receiving a

short, written reply from Robin. So, when I

received a telephone call from his secretary

inviting me to a party at Robin's house, I was

flabbergasted. Robin wanted to talk to me in

person, not only about Cain, but to see if he

could offer any advice about my own writing

projects. I didn't need to ponder my pile of

rejection letters too long—I immediately

accepted.

I arrived at the party bearing an

inscribed copy of my first novel at the time.

As Robin graciously accepted it, he took my

hand and smiled. Having worked in a nursing

home, I knew right away that he had Parkinson's, but he was still sharp and warm and possessed the energy an eighteen-year-old would envy. He showed me around his home, filled with swords, first editions, and framed movie posters from some of his books that had made it to the big screen, like *The Green Berets*, *Inchon*, and *The Happy Hooker*.

I've never been that good mingling in crowds. I usually find a platter of nibble food and pretend to like whatever I find on it, when all I'm doing is seeking a place to hang around while sipping a drink I also pretend to enjoy. Generally, as soon as I find a convenient chance to leave, I bolt out of there so fast you'd think someone had just yelled "Fire!" Robin made me feel welcome though and when I found myself last man standing— more accurately sitting, with Robin in his kitchen, chatting until midnight—I felt surprisingly at ease. We talked about Vietnam, Korea, John Wayne, and Popeye Doyle. As we spoke, figuring this was a "one-shot" deal, I was simultaneously drafting my thank you letter to him, which is why I was genuinely surprised when he invited me back.

This seventy-five-year-old man, whom I had never met before, was soon reading and critiquing my work, encouraging me to push through the rejections and not quit. And he didn't simply preach not quitting, he lived it, full throttle.

Not long after the War with Afghanistan began, Robin, who already had full-blown Parkinson's, paused only long enough to pack little more than a cane, a pen, and a notepad, before traveling to Afghanistan to meet up with the Special Forces. That's where the story was and, if Robin was going to write a book about the War, that's where he was going. A few years later, approaching eighty, Robin jumped on a plane to cover the war with Iraq. Same deal: Parkinson's, pen, notepad, catch a plane, get the story. If there was ever a man who held the patent on not quitting, it was Robin, which is why I thought about him when contemplating joining the Army at forty. As insane as it seemed for me to do this, particularly after battling cancer, per Robin's example, the bottom line kept tallying up the same every time—it could be done. I was forty, cancer free for two years, and the Army accepted recruits up until the age of forty-two. Besides, in the early 1960s, pushing forty himself, Robin trained with the Green Berets in order to prepare for a deployment to Vietnam.

Knowing most would find countless reasons for me not to enlist, I did not tell my brothers, closest friends, or my law partner about my goal. The only people I told were Robin and his wife Helen. By this time, Robin and Helen had moved to Hopkinsville, Kentucky. I flew down to visit them. Robin had developed esophageal cancer and was in the hospital to have a stent placed in his esophagus. Even though he was hospitalized, he seemed peaceful and comforted with his wife Helen by his side. Helen was standing beside him, holding his hand, and cheering him onward. When I leaned over to tell him my plans, I felt confident he heard me. Later I discussed it with Helen, who urged me on with her usual fighting spirit. I left a few days later, worried about leaving my friend Robin, who was still in the hospital, but true to spirit, still fighting the odds.

Shortly after I arrived home, I tracked down a recruiter who happened to be stationed in an armory located in my hometown, Lexington, Massachusetts. He seemed puzzled by my eagerness to enlist.

"Even though you have a college

degree, you're too old to be an officer," he told me. "The cut off for officer training is forty. As an attorney, you might be able to get a direct commission as a JAG."

"I've been working as an attorney for years," I said. "I'd rather enlist."

"What area?"

I shrugged. "I don't know, what areas are there?"

He could tell I'd put a lot of thought into this decision.

He read off some occupational specialties: Chaplain's Assistant, Cook, Combat Engineer.

"Whoa," I said, "what does that entail?"

"Combat Engineers locate IEDs and dispose of them before they dispose of us."

"That sounds good," I said.

Even though I had graduated from college and law school, like all potential recruits, I still had to take and pass a written examination. I'd thought the bar exam would have been the last test I would ever have to take. Now here I was torturing myself with the prospect of studying for another examination. The fear of not passing was almost a deal breaker. I thought you could just join the Army like in the movie *Stripes*.

I calmly asked, "What's the test about?"

"Really just high school stuff. You passed the bar exam. Shouldn't be difficult."

"What kind of high school stuff?"

"Simple math, English, science," he explained. "You won't have a problem. I'll schedule a time for you."

"Right. Sounds easy," I said, lying.

Afterward I double-timed it to a bookstore in Lexington Center and thankfully found a study book, something like *Military Exam Study Guide for Dummies over Forty*. I bought it and studied all the stuff I never learned in high school, like how to divide and multiply fractions, and the true meaning of how the heck 'X really did equal Y.' I learned about amoebas and microbes and discovered that there were different types of life forms, beyond Democrats and Republicans. By test day I was locked and loaded. My number two pencils, lined up, honed, and ready for battle.

When I arrived at the examination room in Springfield, Massachusetts, it didn't resemble the high school rooms I remembered. No desks or chalkboards. No pencil sharpeners or paper test packets. No examination monitors with tight-bunned hair and horn-rimmed glasses. I stood, rather flabbergasted, in a room that housed nothing but computer monitors, and the small workstations each required. Who would've thought the Army was going green?

The administrator must have noticed my befuddled look as she sidled over to me and began using strange words like "log on"; "browser"; and "username." I could feel all the math and science, so delicately and orderly bottled in my brain, spraying out into the atmosphere and being swept away by heavy gusts. I was so rattled that I didn't even know how to take the test, it felt like all the preparation I'd done for tackling its content vanished. My brilliant military career was over before it began. I thought about men like Robin, who spent a good part of his young adulthood as a gunner in the turret ball of a B-17 bomber. In contrast, here I was at the age of forty shell-shocked over a keyboard located within the safe confines of a workstation. I calmed myself and soldiered on. I did my best to ignore the seventeen-year-old guys and gals to my left and right, already clacking away with ease, as if the great American novel were pouring out of them "onto the page."

Methodically, with a click here and a click there, I managed to get through all six sections of the examination, all the while

praying that I was saving my answers

correctly. As soon as we completed the

examination we were instructed to collect our

written results and take them to our recruiter.

All I needed was a thirty-five to pass and all I

wanted to do was pass. I prayed that I'd done

so as I'd clicked "send," which forwarded my

results to the administrator. When I was

directed to report to her front-and-center, she

looked at me and smiled, and then handed me

a folded piece of paper. "Your recruiter is

going to be very happy," she said.

I didn't even look at my grade. I just

made a mad dash to the waiting room, where I handed the paper to my recruiter and held my breath.

"Ninety-four," he said, shaking his head in jest. "What, you couldn't get a hundred?"

My heart thundered with pride. Robin would be impressed.

A few weeks later, I had my medical physical. Since I was over forty it would require two-days in contrast to one day for the younger recruits. I went through an EKG and many other exams humans over forty are reluctant to discuss in mixed company. My final results wouldn't be in for a few days, but

I felt certain I'd get the call. Amazingly, I breezed through, but it was anti-climactic since a few days before the physical I'd received word from Helen that Robin had passed away.

The day after my physical, I flew down to Kentucky to attend Robin's wake and funeral. Throughout the flight, I would think: "I can't wait to tell Robin I enlisted." Then a split second later I would recall the purpose of my visit.

Robin now rests by his parents' side in Sleepy Hollow Cemetery located in Concord, Massachusetts and not too far from

Concord's most brilliant citizens: the Hawthornes, Alcotts, Thoreaus, and Emersons. Robin is, in my book, at home among the great Concord Idealists.

I like to believe that Robin knows I enlisted and served honorably. Still, I wished more than anything that I could have shared the experience with my friend and mentor. I often longed for his reassuring pat on the back or a few tips about Army life. Still, I know that we'll *rendezvous* someday. In the meantime, I'll soldier on and offer my own pat on the back and some useful tips to new recruits or struggling authors. I owe Robin, and the veterans who taught me how to swing

a hammer and pen a phrase, at least that

much—and more.

***

TEN

Asses and Elbows

The vocation of every man and woman
is to serve others.
–Tolstoi

I can still hear and picture my boss Bud

Foley tearing me a new one that Monday

morning in August 1985. "It's asses and

elbows here on the weekends," Bud said to

me, shaking his head more in disappointment than scorn. "All asses and elbows."

Disappointment is how Bud got to you. He didn't need to bark out orders. A certain look or a slight shake of the head usually got your backside in high gear.

I had recently landed a custodial job at Pine Knoll Nursing Home in my hometown, Lexington, Massachusetts. Typically, three custodians would be on duty during the 7 a.m. to 3 p.m. shift. The nursing home consisted of three wings: West, East, and North. Bud oversaw the whole facility, but the East Wing was known as "Bud Country." The day before my "asses-and-elbows" upbraiding from Bud,

I had been assigned to the North wing.

My duties included emptying the trash

bins from each room in the morning, dry

mopping each room and the hallway, wet

mopping the entire wing, and running over

the linoleum floor with the buffer, spray

waxing along the way. In the afternoon, I had

to empty the trash again and then call it a day.

Not a difficult job, still, when you're

seventeen and the only reason you're

punching a clock is to pull together mischief

money, everything's tough about your job—

except collecting your paycheck. I'd cut a few

corners that previous Sunday and Bud decided to let me know Monday morning, that things didn't pass muster.

Bud looked exactly like someone named Bud Foley should look like—cropped silver hair, broad shoulders, thick forearms, hands that could palm a hot engine block, and thick, black-rimmed glasses. Bud had a habit of removing his glasses during important conversations and then using them as a veteran trial attorney might, while schooling a jury. His head, far too big for even his broad shoulders, contained more facts, figures, and street knowledge than a National Security

Agency computer bank. Most importantly,

Bud had a light blue, button-up shirt with the

name "Bud" embroidered in navy-blue,

threaded script over his left breast pocket, a

pocket that always contained at least two pens

and a notepad. I coveted one of those

custodian shirts, but deep down I knew my

custodian skills were as limited as my

enthusiasm for the work. Even at seventeen,

my instincts told me I'd never be important

enough to wear one of those shirts.

Bud wore his shirt, as you might

imagine, tucked into his blue-collar trousers,

whose pressed trouser cuffs lightly brushed

his spit-polished work boots. Bud was a World War II, Korean War, and Viet Nam-era veteran, but if you spoke to Bud, you would have sworn he'd lived a charmed life.

As Bud took corrective action over me we stood outside his East Wing custodial closet, its door wide open. I can still smell the "Blue Chip" floor cleaner we used, and see one of the medium-coarse, red buffer pads we used. We would spray wash them with the hunk of garden hose attached to the slop-sink nozzle located in the closet. Afterward, we would hang the pad onto the nozzle to drip dry.

Bud's closet was a source of pride. He kept everything in it ship-shape. Squared away. A place for everything and everything in its place. If one needed a screwdriver, Phillips or flathead, or a quarter-inch wing-nut, one knew exactly where to locate it in Bud's custodial locker. The water in his mop bucket was always fresh and at the ready for the next cranberry juice spill or other accidents of nature.

At the moment I had to face Bud's wrath, I felt like an accident of nature myself. I'd blown off emptying the trash that Sunday. He knew it. I knew it. "What's asses and elbows mean?" I asked, as if Bud owed my punk, know-it-all self an answer.

He gave me the look. "You guys sit on your asses all weekend here and, when you're not, you're leaning on your elbows. Asses and elbows. Every one of you. None of these people live here by choice. This is their last stop in life. The least you can do is police the area before you punch out and empty their trash. Give 'em some dignity."

I can't say I had an epiphany, but I got the message. Bud taught me other important things, too, like how to plunge a toilet, wring a wet mop properly, change a patient's oxygen tank, and, when at all possible, never lead with a five while playing cribbage. He also taught me to practice using my weak hand—in my case, my left—when doing small chores, like using a screwdriver, banging a nail, or fastening a bolt.

"You build up your agility that way," Bud would explain. "Never know when you might have to use your left hand. Work towards making it as good as your right."

Three decades later, I think of Bud when I attack a Phillips head screw with my left hand, sometimes just for the hell of it, and sometimes because my left still needs practice.

During the growing seasons, the Pine Knoll custodial crew would also be tasked with landscaping the home's courtyard. Bud taught me that there's nothing random about mowing a lawn. "Keep the lines straight, cross cut it, don't go too fast or you'll leave stragglers, keep the blade sharp or you'll tear the blades of grass instead of cutting them, and don't cut it in the same pattern every time or it will make ruts in the lawn," he'd instruct.

He also insisted we compost the clippings—going green long before jet-setters found it trendy. He expected us to use the same expert care while trimming the hedges, weeding and edging the beds, and making sure the annuals exhibited plenty of pluck.

"This may be the only outside world these people will ever see again," he would say, not preaching, just in passing. "Let's make it look good."

After college, I worked in the healthcare field for a couple of years and then started a landscaping business while attending law school at night. That business covered most of my tuition. More than that, the physical work and the pride of a job well done kept me sane while I struggled through difficult points of law.

Bud earned his degree from the school of continuous education, from institutions of higher learning, called serving in the Navy, surviving multiple wars, firefighting, being a husband, rearing children, surviving a double bypass, and now being a dedicated custodian. During lunches, he taught me how to interpret stock data in the newspaper, and introduced me to reading and pondering editorials and discussing current events with coworkers and friends. They taught none of this stuff in college. I owned no stocks, had no worthy opinions, and the only current event I had any real interest in worked in the kitchen and she had no interest in me. Still, I felt quite the intellectual teenager thumbing through the newspaper while sipping my morning joe with my "WW II buddies," Bob, Dick, and of course, Bud.

We were policing the area one afternoon when Bud stopped me to talk about his double bypass. (He was really telling me that smoking is bad for you.) "They rushed me right past here," he said, pointing to the West Wing nurses' station. "Massive heart attack. That was five years ago. The doctors told me it was only good for five years."

Bud was fifty-nine at the time, but was

still a rock. It wasn't lost on me, however, that

he'd used up his five years and then some.

After his heart attack, Bud had quit smoking

the non-filtered Pall Malls he'd choked on

since "the Big Two." He was a skier, a hiker,

and an educator now. Not always the case, but

he had, long ago, quit the booze.

He once told a story from his Navy

days. "Guys picked me to go on a milk run,

and I don't know what go into to me, but I

took the milk money, hopped on a flight, and

went off on a toot for a week. They ripped me

a new one when I finally returned."

As a teenager, I had no idea what the

hell Bud was talking about, or even what the hell prompted this confession. Bud's stories frequently came with no introduction. They would t-bone you out of nowhere, begin somewhere in the second act, and contain sayings not used since the Dodo bird first appeared on the scene. After some skillful cross examination I figured out that his Navy buddies gave him a wad of cash to buy booze—"milk money"—and that Bud used it to go on a solo binge. This was his way of lecturing me about alcohol abuse, which eventually soaked in after my first battle with cancer. It's been eleven years since I've blown any milk money.

Bud was big on taking care of your own little corner of the world. He was officially a custodian at the home, but it wasn't unusual to see Bud taking on "nursing" duties like tying an elderly lady's shoe, finding an extra blanket, spooning some Cream of Wheat their way, or asking them to save a dance for him.

He always carried a small putty knife in his back pocket. "Let's police the halls, Mac," he'd say, pointing down the hallway. I felt like I'd earned a modicum of respect when he called me "Mac." He'd whip out his putty knife and we'd patrol the halls, searching for, and finding, microscopic specs of dirt on the floor. The putty knife made short work of the little offender foolish enough to blemish Bud Country. "You could eat off my floors," Bud boasted often. We never did eat off of them, but I got the message: No task too big. No task too small. Attention to detail is always important.

The first time Bud taught me how to use the floor buffer nearly ended with me leveling the place. While demonstrating how it was done, Bud held a mug of black coffee in his right hand and used his left (his weak hand) to control the buffer with ease. He told me to give it a whirl. Based on how he handled it, I thought it'd be a stroll in the park; but when I latched both hands onto the buffer's handle, the machine immediately spun out of control. The evil contraption hurled me into the wall, the handle bruising my ribs before flying off into the baseboard, punching a substantial hole through the sheetrock. My immediate reaction, after complete and utter embarrassment, was that—if he could handle this bull one-handed—this old guy must be the toughest guy in the world.

Bud laughed and then showed me a few

artful tricks on how to control the beast.

Afterward, he taught me how to repair

sheetrock holes. Within a few days, I became

a buffing master and, like Bud, I could soon

buff one-handed—righty or lefty. I got so

good I could've buffed the inside of shoebox

without clipping the sides. And you can be

damn sure that when the pretty nurses' aides

walked by me, I switched to one-handed

buffing to show off my talent. I never

received any specific feedback from the ladies,

but undoubtedly they were impressed.

In all honesty, I'm still proud of my

buffing skills, and all the little skills Bud

taught me, which did more than help me clean up. While attending law school, I also earned serious bank working for a hardwood flooring company. Towards the end of the summer, the flooring company cleaned dorm room floors by the score at Harvard University. In a mad rush to get the rooms in ship-shape order before school began, our team would get cranking at 6:00 a.m. and work twelve-hour days. I would spend the entire day whipping the buffer from one room into the next, screening off the dirt and grime in preparation for the crew behind me. A buddy followed behind with a vacuum and another followed him applying a fresh coat of polyurethane. We had it, as they say, down to science, and I always enjoyed passing on the skills Bud taught me.

I was forty-one when I entered Army basic combat training. Most of the men and women I trained with were eighteen or nineteen, and the drill sergeants made me the barracks leader, on Day One, which meant it was my job to make sure our barracks were spic and span. This meant daily dry mopping, wet mopping, and buffing the linoleum floors. The United States Army never knew what hit 'em.

I taught my crew how to wring a wet mop properly—twist the mop head in the wringer and then squeeze it dry. By twisting the head to compact it, you're able to make it drier, which means, the floor doesn't get as wet as you mop, will dry quicker, and will be ready for buffing much sooner. When you're done with the mop bucket, dump out the dirty water, and fill it up with fresh water. Clean the wax build up off the buffing pads after each use. I also taught the young ones how to double-line the trash barrels so there's always a second trash bag on deck, and to keep the custodial closet organized, so when the drill sergeants order an unexpected clean-up party (a.k.a. "G.I. party") we wouldn't be left holding our asses in our hands looking for stuff. "Always plan ahead," I schooled them.

In basic training, our bay had a white board we could use. As bay leader, I developed a system where each week I would write on the board the name of a dry mop captain, wet mop captain, buffing captain, and trash captain. Each captain oversaw his respective tasks and would have to coordinate with the other captains in order to get his job done. Each captain would also have two subordinates below him to assist; hence, teaching them chain-of-command skills and principles.

The next week I would rotate the crewmembers in order to give everyone a taste of what it was like to be on different ends of the food chain. By the end of basic training, the drill sergeants would matter-of-factly shout out things like, "Mac where's the dry mop captain?" or "Who's the wet mop captain, Mac?" as if this system had always been in place. As with Bud, when the drill sergeants called me "Mac," I felt like I'd won their respect. I wonder sometimes whether they adopted the chain-of-command cleaning system I created. At minimum, in the fall of 2008, at Fort Jackson, South Carolina—nearly twenty-five years after I met him and almost seven decades after his own basic training— Bud Foley's custodial standards were alive and well at the Foxtrot Company 2/13 Infantry Regiment.

When I left Pine Knoll in the fall of 1990, after becoming a big-fancy-ass college graduate, I lost track of Bud even though we lived in the same town. I always meant to look him up, but never did. Not too long ago I ran into a firefighter in town and as we chatted, I asked him if he knew of a former firefighter named Bud Foley. "No," he said, "but I've heard of him. I think that guy died."

It's tough to think of Bud being reduced to "that guy," but who am I to judge the firefighter who characterized Bud this way? I'm "that guy" who never called on Bud for a quick game of cribbage, or to get his take on the latest election results, or for a good stock tip. God knows I could use one.

Too often, when we move on, we tend to leave the mentors in our lives behind, somehow assuming we'll be able to pull them out of the bottom of a metaphorical toolbox whenever we want. We tell ourselves lies, like we could, at a moment's notice, still put our hands on a quarter-inch wing nut in the East Wing custodial closet. The truth: we often let the quiet village heroes who took an active role in raising us—for no other reason than it was the right thing to do—slip away, without so much as a thank you, a quick note to let them know we made it through, or even so much as a spoonful of Cream of Wheat before their last dance.

Sometimes I overhear these middle-aged clichés sitting around with nothing but spent milk money sagging over their waists, complaining about alimony, child support, and the decline of American ingenuity. In between "milk runs" of their own, they praise great men like Harold "Bud" Foley and then lament how "they don't make 'em like they used to." All I can think of is asses and elbows. Asses and elbows.

***

ELEVEN

The Accidental Caretaker

Part II

Ruth "Mom" McAleer

The best things are the most difficult.
—Ancient Greek Proverb

Until cancer got its venomous fangs

into her, my mother had been a world-

champion "doer." She was always doing

something. Whether reading, teaching,

knitting, weeding, swimming, planning,

coaching basketball, cooking, polishing, entertaining, plumbing, solving newspaper mind twisters, rearing baby boomers and latch-key kids, attending dad's functions, writing checks for one women's auxiliary club after another, or searching for the bright side of every mishap, my mother kept busy.

In classic 1940s and 1950s photos, my mother resembled a Hollywood beauty with a silver-screen smile and long, thick, wavy black hair. She was thin, hardy, and radiated youth, long after that era considered any unmarried woman over twenty-one a spinster. Her loves included teaching, skiing, coaching girls' high-school basketball, driving, swimming, and diving. She was thirty-two when my father finally "caught her" on December 28, 1957.

After two full-term miscarriages in the late 1950s, my mother went on to spend most of the 1960s pregnant, thanks to the infamous "wonder drug Diethylstilbestrol" commonly known as DES. It was a female hormone used to prevent miscarriages—eventually discontinued when it was linked to causing cancer and reproductive abnormalities. My mother dismissed the idea of litigation. "I don't believe in suing people who are trying to help you," she'd say, referring to her obstetrician.

She was forty-two when I bounced onto the scene, yet I knew her as a mother who had given up her body and physical youth, but not her spirit, to eight pregnancies.

The mother I knew loved the underdog and had a genius for identifying the kid in the neighborhood who needed a lift and then finding a way to boost his confidence. She despised bullies and also had a genius for putting them in their place—by being brutally honest. A penny never passed through her hands she didn't work twice as hard to earn. She once told me how her father broke his leg on the job during the Great Depression and refused to collect worker's compensation. He didn't believe in getting paid for not working and was afraid it would come out of his co-workers' pockets. He had five mouths to feed at the time, which neither he, nor my mother, saw as a reason to accept what they saw as charity.

To my everlasting annoyance, my mother knew every rule of table etiquette and drilled them into our heads. *Spoon your soup away from you . . . Keep one hand on your lap . . . Elbows off the table . . .* she'd say. Mom also knew how to talk turkey. When it came time to barter with plumbers, electricians, car mechanics, or fix the disposal with the end of a broom handle, my father knew that my mother had him beat, by at least a couple of furlongs, and gladly stepped aside.

After her youngest—this writer— entered kindergarten in 1972, Mom resumed teaching high school full time. She taught business and typing until she retired in 1987. Only a few years later, Mom began dedicating most of her time to taking care of my father after he was diagnosed with non-Hodgkin's lymphoma. It seems sacrifice was another thing my mother did very well. She insisted on spending most of her retirement money on

her six kids and eight grandchildren. Looking

back, I'm not the slightest bit surprised that

she never told anybody about the lump she

found probably sometime in early 2002. Mom

had bigger things on her mind like the small

problems of others.

When her primary care doctor felt the

lump, he sent her to the hospital for tests. As

she'd likely suspected—and kept to herself—

she had breast cancer. She still didn't tell

anyone. When I dropped my mother off at

the hospital that morning in March 2002, I

had no idea she was having a single-mastectomy. She'd made it sound as if she were going in for little more than a pedicure.

The mother I picked up that afternoon was not the mother I had kissed goodbye that morning. Rather than being feisty and brimming with energy, this mother seemed like a lifetime of hustle and bustle had finally caught up with her. She didn't even have the strength to negotiate stairs, so I immediately removed the furniture from the dining room and set up a bed, and as many of her special things I could squeeze in, without running the risk that she'd trip over them later. No one assigned me the duty of caretaker. I just happened to be the lucky one there that day and slid into the role because I adored my mother and, for once, she needed me.

Years earlier, anticipating that her older sister Alice would need a place to live, my mother had a small room with a full bath added to the first floor of the house. In this instance, my mother became the benefactor of her own generosity. Here I could shower and bathe my mother in private. Little by little she regained strength, but the first round of chemotherapy sent her into congestive heart failure and into the respiratory intensive care unit for sixteen days.

Though she bounced back eventually, from that point on, my mother seemed happy she didn't have to fight the cure anymore. For the next fourteen months, a wonderful team of homecare helpers and her friend Kathy and I tended to my mother, who was sometimes childlike. One day, as I came downstairs, her hand flitted to her chest as her eyes peered up at me. "Is Daddy dead?" she asked. She didn't calm down until I reassured her that my father was alive and would come down shortly.

The homecare team taught me better ways to walk with her, bathe her, and, among other things, test her blood and inject her insulin. When I came home one day and found my diabetic mother virtually unconscious, I set up a baby monitor in my room and one in hers. This way, I could be upstairs with my father and still be able to hear my mother when she stirred or asked to go the bathroom. Somehow we all muddled through the rough nights. Together.

During these times, I also tended to my mother's hair. After helping her shower and wrapping her in fluffy towels, I'd also rub lotion onto her arms and legs and apply baby powder in places where she undoubtedly sprinkled me with care some thirty-six years earlier. While I could handle those bathing rituals, I didn't feel confident about handling her thick, wavy Hollywood hair, which had gone gray but had not abandoned her since she had only one treatment of chemo.

Luckily, her hairstylist loved my mother and would come to our house every two weeks to wash and style her hair. Often the stylist's husband would come along to chat, making it a social occasion for us all. Every time the stylist leaned my mother over the kitchen sink to wash her hair, I couldn't help but remember how my mother would scold us for attempting to wash our hands over the kitchen sink. "Use the bathroom . . . and use soap," she'd admonish.

For the next two weeks, my mother's hair would be left in my care, and I soon got used to mastering a careful brush here and an artful brush there to bounce the waves into place. Every time I brushed her hair, my mother would look ten years younger, and that's the image I remember even as I held her hand as she took her last breath—a more vibrant, full of sass mother who always put others before herself but also had a zest for life.

***

I don't know why caring for my parents' hair sticks with me years after they passed. One could, I assume, find articles or psychological research that reveals the subconscious meaning behind brushing someone else's hair. To me, caring for their hair was the final step in my efforts to keep them groomed and feeling as strong as possible. Perhaps, I, like Samson, thought their hair reflected their strength, their vibrancy, how alive they'd always felt to me. Maybe there was a part of me that wished the artful arrangement of their thick locks would somehow restore order.

But who cares why, really.

All I know is that those months spent tending to my parents' final days were precious, and often love is better expressed by the simple acts you do, rather than the words you say. It's not a usual thing, one assumes, for a man still in his thirties to embrace taking care of two parents concurrently dying from cancer, but that's what I did, and I was lucky and blessed to have the opportunity to do so. For it was in those moments that I was able to show my parents how much I loved and respected them—one strand of hair at a time.

TWELVE

It Takes a Caravan

Always have time for others and others
will have time for you.
–John McAleer, PhD

I don't necessarily think of myself as a

cancer survivor. It makes it sound like I

slugged it up that long hill under my own

steam. Such a claim would be untrue. I was

just one of the many fighters out there who

helped me beat this thing. My fight simply could not have been won without the caravan of cancer fighters consisting of family, friends, and strangers—some living, some dead—who jumped aboard and made sacrifice after sacrifice to travel the bumpy road with me. As a result, none of the foregoing could have been written or lived without their help. Impossible as it is, my hope now is to offer them all some kind of thank you.

I could capture only a small portion of the generosity and kindness shown to me by my brothers Jay and Paul and Aunt Alice. Jay worked many 1st, 2nd, and 3rd shifts to keep things a going concern at home and Paul kept the place broom clean. My Uncle Robert, who fought his own battle against cancer, commanded the prayer line along with his sister, my Aunt Catherine, my godmother Claire, Father James A. Woods, and my good friends Maureen and Neil.

Always ready to travel were my friends Mrs. McGann, Kathy, Mary J., Vince, Stephanie, Jack, Maureen, Kevin, Jill, Jonathan, Lynne, Peter, Karen, John, Mrs. Rommel, Dot, Bob, Heather, Vinny, Kieran, Jimbo, Donnie, Ana, Grace, Dan, Jean, Nancy M., Doreen, Amy, Jody, Nancy & Dapper,

Frank, Mudd, Tom, Rich, Don P., Paula, Stephen, Moe, James, Shadow, and all my friends and neighbors from Webster Island. My nieces Eileen and Caroline and nephew Liam provided me with a steady stream of reasons to stay in the fight. They, along with my cousins Dawna and John, all kept my cylinders firing with regular visits or prayers and promises of smoother roads ahead.

Others were also front-and-center like my neighbor Doctor Merrifield who inspired me to get a crop of tomato starters going and start caring for something other than myself. His prescription worked and ought to be bottled. My cousin Michael, a strength training coach, regularly offered me little tips to get me back in the driver's seat again and ultimately back on course. My friends Lenny and Barbara made sure my cable TV and DVD player were always stocked with plenty of old movies and some new ones too.

I need, of course, to thank—praise really—the incredible doctors, nurses, health care providers, especially those at MGH, and all those working tirelessly behind the scenes in research and development labs all over the world, who people like me will likely never meet or know.

I have met so many brave and selfless cancer fighters along the way. Sometimes I find myself thinking about the many faces I've seen in the various treatment rooms I've visited, and wonder if this cancer fighter or that cancer fighter made it through. I like to think so. I won't likely ever know, but they're all a part of me now and remain in the fight.

Last, but not least, I must thank my father's World War II battle buddy Elmo Mann. Elmo is a Southern Gentleman who, at age 91, never fails to bring this Yank a cup of cheer (and a good Southern recipe or two) via e-mail, text, or telephone. Being able to still reach out and touch the Greatest Generation has given me more joy, courage, hope, and inspiration than Elmo could ever imagine. So, my final thought for the present: no matter where the road takes you, fuel the caravan with the Elmos in your life and, as a special bonus, they too could live with that.

***

71407467R00131

Made in the USA
Columbia, SC
29 May 2017